wisdom's choice

wisdom's choice

Kathryn Adams Shapiro

Beyond Words Publishing, Inc.
20827 N.W. Cornell Road, Suite 500
Hillsboro, Oregon 97124-9808
503-531-8700
1-800-284-9673

Managing editor: Julie Steigerwaldt
Design: Dorral Lukas
Composition: William H. Brunson Typography Services

Printed in the United States of America
Distributed to the book trade by Publishers Group West

Library of Congress Cataloging-in-Publication Data
Shapiro, Kathryn Adams.
Wisdom's choice / Kathryn Adams Shapiro.
p. cm.
ISBN 1-58270-068-0
1. Healing—Religious aspects. I. Title.

BL65.M4 S465 2002
291.3'1—dc21

2001056558

The corporate mission of Beyond Words Publishing, Inc.:
Inspire to Integrity

To Ron,
to all of our children,
to Love.

Foreword

Wisdom's Choice is the answer to my prayers. It was written through thought impression, every morning, as I sat in prayerful meditation seeking guidance from God and healing for others, as well as myself.

I am a spiritual healer. I work with people who have nowhere else to go for help, because they have been given "no hope" by the medical profession. The day came when I had to turn someone away. That day became a turning point for me.

A woman with a diagnosis of rheumatoid arthritis called to ask for my help. At the time, I was overwhelmed with an extraordinary number of patients. I apologetically explained that I could not take on her case because she did not fit the category of being given "no hope" by a doctor. Her reply—"My doctor has given me 'no hope.' I have 'no hope' of ever being without pain."—still rings in my mind, years later, as I write these words.

My prayers changed that day. I now asked God for healing for others as well as for help specific to my work.

"Dear God, help me to help more people. The need is so great. Spread me out, God. Please give me a way to teach them how to help themselves. I can't reach them all, and it is almost unbearable for me to turn them away. Please God, show me the way."

Every day for several weeks this was my prayer or a variation of it. Then one day, not unlike any other as I sat in prayerful meditation, I received a very clear message in the form of a strong thought. The message was this:

"We will be writing a book together. The name of the book is Wisdom's Choice. *It will be helpful to you if you close your eyes as you write, at least in the beginning. I will tell you when to turn the page and you will leave spaces, as you may choose to add your own thoughts or understanding. The book will be written one day at a*

time. You may choose to write at the same time, or several times, each day. My guidance is always available. It is your choice. I am ready to begin when you are. Trust and it will be so."

I immediately reached for a journal sitting untouched on my desk nearby. At the end of my writing that first day, I closed the journal and read its previously unseen title, "One Day at a Time." I sat for quite a while, overwhelmed with emotions of love and gratitude. I was in a profound state of awe as I asked, "What is your name, or is your name not important for me to know at this time?" My answer was this:

"I Am the Source of Love. God is what you would call Me. Others call Me what feels right to them, in accordance with their own understanding. Thank you for this time together to help yourself and others. We will begin each day as we left off. You will see. You will learn Trust. Ask and you shall receive. These are new beginnings for all living things.

I Love You."

Later, I asked for guidance about whether or not to include my personal understanding of the messages received. What became clear to me was that each of us, at any given time, will take from this guidance whatever we need. Many—and perhaps all—of the passages, will have different meanings for each individual reader. The book can be read from front to back, or opened at any page, for daily guidance and inspiration when you seek answers.

Quiet your mind, and allow yourself to receive the gift of guidance. You will feel what is right for you. Whatever meaning you take from the reading is your personal message at that time. Your guidance may change with subsequent readings. Change is growth. Only God is constant. Understand that the very thing that God "needs" is exactly what we need—a true relationship with Him.

Note:
The use of He throughout the book was chosen for its universal meaning and is not

intended to assign gender. God is All. There can be no limitation imposed on God.

Minimal editing has been done to achieve, as closely as possible, the authenticity of the original passages. Personal references and entries have been omitted, and therefore, some parts of the book may seem disjointed to the reader. For this, I apologize.

—Kathryn Adams Shapiro

one

You chose to come here. You have a Plan. You may choose to remember the Plan and choose whether or not to enact the Plan within this lifetime. There are no accidents or mistakes. Everything is according to Plan. You need only to remember. The way to remember is found by going within, not outside yourself. Quiet your mind religiously and the answers will come. Trust and it will be so. Your intention creates your focus. It does not happen overnight. Be patient. Be calm. The answers are already there; you need only to retrieve them. They come from God, the Source of All, just as you do. There is nothing Real that is not of God. If it is of evil, it is your physical mind that has brought it into being. Your own physical mind is its creator, source, not God.

I Love You.

TWO

You must trust that our connection cannot be broken. This is not possible. The connection lives forever. Even when the Life Force leaves the physical body, the connection to Me, The Source, lives on. The body is temporal. It is the temple that holds the Soul for an experience on the earth plane.

This is the Plan we talked of earlier. The Soul chooses what lessons it needs to learn while on earth. The body is chosen, the parents are chosen, all circumstances supporting the lesson are chosen by the Soul and others it agrees to have this earth experience with. Yes, this means those you consider to be your worst enemies, and those you may call your Soul mates. They are, each of them, your Soul mates.

Everything is carefully chosen to support the Soul's unending quest for enlightenment and True understanding of the Oneness of

All, God. There are experiences your personality does not comprehend the True meaning of. Your personality, your physical mind, cries out, "Why me?" and sometimes blames God for that which you do not remember was agreed upon as necessary for the growth of your Soul. You may believe that I have used these experiences to punish you. I do not punish. I Love unconditionally. I Am Love.

Understand that you *are* Spirit, experiencing life on the physical plane, not a human being having a spiritual experience such as the one who writes these words. This is an experience within a lifetime, not the Life itself. The Life Force is of Spirit. It is from the Source of Life, All That Is. Your mind is of God Mind, One with the Universe. Your brain is of your physical body.

Wisdom comes from your connection with God, Truth. Knowledge is what you can fill your brain with while in the physical experience. Choose Wisdom. Choose Truth. Consciously connect with The Source and your life will be of joy, forever.

Love is all there is. I Am Love. Nothing else matters, nothing else is eternal. Truth is Love. You and I are One. I Am One with All That Is. The connection cannot be broken. I Am Life. I Am Love.

I Love You.

Three

What is Truth? It is that which you know to exist within the core of your being. It is individual according to the Soul's path of development. When you hear or read or speak that which elicits a bodily response, a knowing, you may say, "That rings true for me." You *know* Truth on an intuitive level.

It is important for you to honor Truth by applying it in your daily life. It is the act of bringing your Truth forth in outward expression that is what you came here to do, to create your Truth in physical form. That is why earth is called the physical plane or realm. You are here to manifest into physical form that which you *know* within your Soul to be your individual Truth. If all of you were to accomplish this, just imagine the symphony the God of your Universe would be directing. This is the goal.

Each of you, like your fingerprints, is unique, but created by and connected to the same Source. This is for good reason. There is a Plan. Trust and you will know that you are playing your part as directed.

Simple truths and simple acts can produce profound results. Consider the last drop, joining others like it in a cup, yet it is the one to enact the overflow. Change can be as simple as that. People fear change, but those thoughts are of their physical mind, not God Mind. God Mind connects you to your reason for being, your Soul's mission, and the inter-relatedness of every living thing.

All parts are essential to the Plan. None is greater or lesser than another. Each of you must do your part to achieve happiness in life. Trying to live someone else's life is trying to play their part, not the one you were designed to play. This brings chaos where beauty was intended. Many on earth at this time prefer to play another's part or do not even consider that they have a part, other than the one their earth mind has chosen to be the best.

Take a lesson from the beauty and harmony of nature, the rhythm of the waves, the balance of the tides with the earth and the moon, the cycles of the seasons, the pollinating of the flowers by the bees, the trees and the important role they play in the air you breathe. All living things in nature are playing out the role intended for them in this lifetime. Imagine now that the same Plan with its perfect execution exists for all people on earth, uniquely designed for them as a part of the Whole.

You did come with instructions, but some of you do not remember. The way to remember is to go within. Silence your physical mind and hear only the guidance from your Source, the God of the Universe. This is the only path to true happiness. The only way to live a joyful life is to attune to your own intuition and then act on it. Beautiful creative ideas are just that, until the artist applies the medium to the surface of what is to be created.

Listen only to your Source; your individual answers can only be found within. Inspiration can be found in others, but you are the creator of your own life. This is all according to Plan. Choose Trust always over fear. Choose Love repeatedly. Bring joy into your own life and the life of others around you. This is the Way.

I Am Love, and you are created in My Likeness. Bring Love forward in your life, and it will truly be said, "On earth as it is in heaven." So Be It.

I Love All of Creation, which came from Love. Like creates like and this continues on, for Eternity.

I Love You.

Four

You create with your thoughts. You choose your thoughts. This is of utmost importance to remember because you are creating your life experience, one thought at a time. You are made in My Likeness—you are a Creator. Know that this is Truth. Change your thinking, change your life.

No one individual or group of individuals is above another. Some people group individuals according to what they think is correct. They group them in a particular race, religion, or skin color and think that one is above another. This is a false teaching that many carefully and systematically perpetuate. This is wrong thinking and you, the writer and the reader, are among the many who are trying to undo this falseness. There is no mistake that you are reading this book, at this time.

All of my children are created equal. All have free will to choose their thoughts, and their thoughts create their reality. Change is possible. Change is necessary. The rewards are great. Realizing this and acting it out in your life, in thought, word, and deed, creates a more fulfilling life in every way. This is eternalizing your Truth. It lives on within you, forever. Do not ever be afraid to lead by example of this Truth. Each Soul has different needs, which you may call lessons, to help them identify with their own Soul's Truth. Each of you came here to find your Truth *and* to bring it into outward expression in your life. The second half of this equation is just as important as the first. This is Wholeness.

I Love You.

Five

What if I were to tell you that the sky is not the separation of heaven and earth? Would you believe this to be so, or would you believe everything you have read or seen in pictures or told to be so as a child?

I do not sit on a throne up in the sky deciding whether or not you will have a life that pleases you. Your relatives and loved ones departed from you only in body do not abide up in the sky with Me, either. Rather, we are All energy and energy takes on many forms. We are as close as your hands and feet, but you may not believe this because you cannot see with your physical sight that which I tell you is True. Many of you even fear this thought, but the reason behind your fear is that it is unfamiliar to you. Would you flee from the one you grieve so much were you to be given the chance to see clearly?

Life lives on after the death of the physical body. Energy takes on new form, but True Love, or Life, goes on forever. I do not speak of the love many of you believe to be the only expression. This is love expressed as feeling. The Love I Am is unconditional. Love Is; love is temporal.

Your thoughts can be adjusted. It is your choice. Choose Love. Open your mind to receive God Truth, and it will be so. Do not fear what you do not see. Open your heart and your mind to see clearly that which is Truth, that which is Love, that which Lives on, forever.

I Love You.

SIX

All of Life is connected. Human mind does not see how this is so. The physical mind concerns itself with the removal of any resources humans think they require for their own consumption or material gain. They see no connection with the way they deplete the earth and the imbalance this creates in nature. They call catastrophic events "acts of God." This is their false truth, which they believe to serve their purpose and fulfill their own desires.

The rivers and streams, the air you breathe, all of nature, are living things and every living thing is connected as a Whole. Imbalance in thinking creates imbalance in nature just as imbalance in human thought creates imbalance, or dis-ease, in the human body. Everything begins with thought. What you would say is good and what you would say is evil, you create with your thoughts. You are made in the Likeness of your Creator. Think it so and it becomes.

You have only the concept of space and time. You do not comprehend the full Life of the Soul. You do not see what came before or what will be. You do not yet understand Cause and Effect. Ignorance of a Truth does not make it false. Truth Is Truth. Truth Is.

I Love You.

seven

Too many live in the past or try to project the future. You continually think and re-think the past, and therefore are living and re-living the past. There is only now, the present moment, which you can create in any way your thoughts imagine.

Image-in (imagine) is another way thought can be used to create. Visualize in your mind that which you want. "See" yourself already receiving that which you long for in your life. Be patient, quietly wait, and know that it *will* come forth. Your mind is a powerful tool. It is used to express into physical form that which you believe to be true.

Watch your thoughts carefully. They hold the key to where your life is going. Thought manifests into physical form. This is true of any creation. The artist's sculpture or the musician's symphony begins with a thought.

Your action, or outward expression in your life, has as its basis whatever truth you hold in your mind. Your life becomes an outward expression of your thoughts. Thoughts of anger or fear create their likeness. Thoughts of love and mercy create their likeness. Thoughts of disease and separation from the Life Force create their likeness. Thoughts of health and wholeness, connection to the Source, All That Is, create a harmonious, beautiful life. You are created in My Likeness, Perfection. It is a joy forever to be at One with your Creator.

I Love You.

eight

Everyone is unique, created in My Likeness, but unique in his or her individuality. Each has his or her own Plan. This Plan, which encompasses everything the Soul came here to learn, may or may not include the experience of a particular religion or way of worshipping God.

This is so because each Soul is unique and may have chosen a particular way of worship or a certain religion to join like-minded spirits in order to share a group thought experience. This can be true of any organization where closed thinking is a prerequisite for the group. I do not mean this in a judgmental way. I do not judge. You judge.

Think about it. If you belong to such a group, organized or not, religious or social, do you not restrict your thoughts in at least some way? Isn't this in fact a defining goal for the group when it was created? Being truthful with yourself, you may have to agree. Some go to extremes in their closed mindedness, and decide for themselves that theirs is the only way to Me. They surround themselves with others who are of like mind to reinforce their "righteousness."

There are as many paths to Me as there are Souls. Each is unique, no one better than another, no way preferred by Me. Each must find the Truth for themselves, within themselves. Each must find his or her personal Truth and bring it into outward expression. This may or may not involve organized religion. For some it will. Do not judge. I do not judge. Find your own way and respect others as they try to do the same.

I Love You.

nine

You are what you think. Your thoughts create the moment, and moments strung together become a lifetime. A single thought can make a difference. Everything created, manifested into physical form, begins with a thought. Single thoughts are easier to change than a cluster of thoughts. Try to change the tone of your thinking before several thoughts are set into motion.

Your perception is your reality. If you can change your thoughts before they consume your thinking in a negative way, you can change your perception and thereby change your reality. You will create positive energy instead of negative around you.

It will not happen overnight, but by changing a single thought, you can take the first step toward changing your life. You will create joy in your life where there was sorrow. You will create hope where there was fear. You are taking control of your life when you thought that your life was beyond your control.

Apply this to every aspect of your own life where you see a need for change. Look at your circumstances and the people in your life in a more positive way. Find one thing, in the beginning, that is good about your present circumstances and those you are in relationships with. Try to let go of your judgments and see good where you thought it was absent. Ask God, the Higher Power of your own Truth, to help you.

It is worth the effort you put forth. You will receive as much as you give. Try to remember this. This is the way to a more abundant life. I do not speak of wealth, as you may think of it, but this Principle can be applied to all aspects of your life.

I want for you that which is Good. This only is Truth. Believe, for It Is So. I Am the Source of Love, I Am the Source of Good, I Am the Source of Light. I Bless you with Love and Light. This Is Truth, not perception.

I Love You.

Ten

I believe that it would be useful to bring further clarity to the significant issue of thought. Try to remember that thoughts are things. Thought manifests into physical form, in the likeness of its creator. In other words, like a flower or a weed grows from its root or source, what you think is what you produce.

Thoughts of love, mercy, compassion, forgiveness, patience, understanding, health, wholeness, joy, and happiness produce like-minded thoughts to return to their creator. Similarly, thoughts of anger, blame, resentment, hate, prejudices, judgment, dishonesty, jealousy, and revenge return to their source in kind.

You have a choice. Always. You are the creator. You have a choice, also, in what you believe to be true. You can accept other people's truths for your own, but you will be receiving another's beliefs, which causes you confusion within your being. This is choosing human consciousness. You are aligning with half-truths and falsehoods along with, yes, some temporal truth, when you choose man-made thoughts and beliefs.

To achieve your highest good, in all aspects of your life, you must choose only God Consciousness, Eternal Truth, Everlasting Wisdom. It is your choice and no one else's. Do not think that I can force this Truth on anyone. Always, there is free will. Always, you must choose. This is Principle/Law. This is Truth.

You can choose the Wisdom and Guidance from God and have joy in your life, or you can choose knowledge from man, which leads to frustration, and sometimes chaos. Your life is intended to align with Perfection. It is a simple but profound decision, and only you can choose.

Every thought matters. Think on this and know that you continually choose, in every moment, how your life will be created by each and every powerful thought. Start to notice where your thoughts come from. God is Pure. God is Good. Nothing but Good originates from God. Know this to be True.

I Love You.

eLeven

Heed the warning of your Soul to act not in haste when judging another's circumstance. The human eye sees myopically, the Soul sees the view of many universes spanning all time, as you have known it. Remember the half-truths and falsehoods of human thinking and use your higher consciousness to guide you, always.

You bring forth in your life that which you give away. I am not speaking of what you call charity, here. I am speaking, again, of your thoughts, so that you will remember their importance. When you judge, you are trying to live another's life. You are avoiding your own. You came here to fulfill your Plan, no one else's. Remember this.

You will be happier with your own life when you create harmony with others. Be the one to reflect My Light within you, so that others may be inspired to do the same. You will live a better life and so will they. You change and others around you change. The Light spreads and harmony replaces chaos.

You choose, in every moment, with every thought. This is so. See the Light and act on It. This is what you came here to do. This is why you are reading this book. You are ready. The time is now.

A beautiful, harmonious life awaits you and those you love. Here and now. Today. You need only to change your thinking from fear and anger to Love and Light, your individual understanding of God. This is the Way.

I Am the Light. This Truth is forever. Choose Love.

I Love You.

Twelve

"Where will I go when I die?" you ask. There are many different realities for each. "Death" is a state of consciousness rather than a destination. You create your experience on this plane with your thoughts, just as on earth your thoughts create your life. On this side, everything you experience is created by thought. There is no need for verbal communication, only thought. That is why the subject of thought is so carefully considered in this writing.

You bring the sum total of your thinking to this side because that is what you are in reality. Do you not see the importance of considering these things before you move into this reality?

This realm is very much like earth in that way. Each of you will reside on a plane in relation to your growth. Remember, none is greater or lesser, but one individual's reality is not another's. Those with a similar reality reside together. The environment you experience is that which you make it with your thoughts.

What you desire (needs are no longer of importance) is what you create by thinking it so. This can be beauty and serenity, or fear and other forms of human thinking that the Soul brings with It. You are what you think. Are you beginning to understand this crucial point we are working with in this writing?

Except for non-verbal communication, many will experience this plane to be very much like earth. In fact, many do not realize that they have left the physical plane except for this phenomenon. So think on this one teaching as the most important. Begin to change your thinking and you will see for yourself how your life and those around you will change. Practice makes perfect. It is important. It takes your time.

This is your life. It is of your design. You create your life with your thoughts. What you become in life, your personality, who you are, lives on after you "die."

It is easier for the Soul to grow while on earth, because you do not experience the resistance or challenges, as you may call them, here on this plane. This is why I urge you to think on this.

Connect with your Source, Pure Thought. Choose My Wisdom over what you have learned from others to be true. I Am Truth. I Am Love.

I Love You.

Thirteen

In the stillness of your mind, you will find your connection to your Source. This is where you will receive answers to the questions you ask of others outside yourself. Each of you has your own personal Truth that connects you to All That Is Truth, your Source, Creator, Universal Mind, The One, All That Is. There are as many names for Me, as you can discover to relate to.

The important point is the connection. This is the Life Force that brings to you the stamina, strength to live Life to your fullest potential. It is the never-ending, always-present supply of Energy that every living thing needs to sustain life, as you know it. It is when this connection to the body is broken that physical life ends and a new state of consciousness, awareness begins. Make no mistake by trying to examine My use of your words or language. The Soul Lives Forever.

I speak only of "death" to the physical body that has temporarily housed your Spirit. Do not succumb to the temptation of fitting My use of words to support your human thought.

You will learn on the next plane of existence that communication by thought is the higher form. Your language is open to interpretation, because many have their own state of awareness concerning certain words and their use. This is further complicated by differences with voice inflection and the charging with emotion of words by the speaker, as well as the receiver's own memories.

Thought transference is the pure form of communication because the thought is directly given and received without need of interpretation. This is how you will discover Life to be on the next plane. No thought is hidden—your personal Truth is known by all. You create your life on the next plane as you do on this one—with your thoughts. The only difference is that on earth you are unaware of this Truth.

You do not believe that which is hidden from your five senses. In fact, you have senses beyond those known to you, but this Truth is hidden from you by your own thinking or state of consciousness. Because of this, you remain unaware of much that could help guide you in your life.

You must open to Truth, not the half-truths of your present existence. All that is necessary to achieve this is to open your mind to the possibility. Open your heart to resonate with this Truth. Ask for clarity in your thinking and you shall receive. Know that this is given to you, as you ask. Align yourself with Truth, and All will be Well. Do not worry.

I Love You.

fourteen

What you think, you believe, and it becomes. It is your choice what you believe. It has always been so. Nothing exists outside of your own mind. Your heart and mind work together. You say, "I know this to be true in my heart."

Your heart is your compass for your life. I use the word compass for intuition, your inner guide, your connection to your Source, the One God of All.

Believe in yourself and All that you are. You are Spirit. You create your life with thoughts. There is one continuous Life everlasting.

Choose a strong connection with your Creator. Only you can break the connection by choosing separation. Ask and you shall receive. Re-build this connection and you shall See. This is Truth. This is Love.

I Love You.

Fifteen

Pure Truth is that which comes from your Higher Self, another word for your Soul. It is your connection to the Source and cannot be broken. When you are in touch with who you are, your True Self, you are in harmony with Truth. You may say that you resonate with this as truth, or that you *know* it to be True. This knowingness comes from within. There is a never-ending supply of guidance available to all for the asking.

This is a Truth too simple for many of you to believe. You want it proven to you with scientific equations and research papers and studies, or to see it with your own eyes. You only believe man-made "truths," which often you do not realize to be half-truths or non-truths. Let your Source validate these truths before accepting them as your Truth.

Ask and you shall receive. The question can be of any subject. Your concern is Mine.

Let Me help you with your life. Only then will you be Living. You will be Alive with Spirit. You will change and others around you will change as well. Choose Pure Truth. Choose to Live. Choose Love.

I Love You.

SIXTEEN

Focus and intention are two very necessary actions to engage Higher Wisdom, Truth. They can be interchangeable in their order. In other words, you can intend something and then your focus will enhance or diminish that which you intend, depending on the amount of focus you give it. The same is true of focus. If you intend sharp focus, using your will to do so, this will be your outcome. Casual or hazy focus produces the same vague intention. Accomplishment requires intention and focus, strengthened by your will, which is your choice.

Everything comes back to choice. You first choose to focus on a certain thing, whether it be an object or emotion. You strengthen what returns to you by the intention you put behind your focus. Your free will is always present and at your command, whether you choose to be conscious of this fact, or not.

On some level you are aware and you have chosen or it would not be so. Consider this carefully. Choose, consciously, where you place your focus. Intention will follow or lead depending on the choice you have made. Do you see the connection here with our focus on thought earlier? They are intertwined. Focused thoughts are sent out to your world and, yes, the next world by your intention.

Strong emotion, negative or positive, strengthens the intention, and adds the energy necessary to manifest your object of focus into physical form. This is the process with which you create your life on a daily basis. Remember, it is your choice. Choose carefully.

I Love You.

seventeen

Remembering that you are a Spiritual being first and foremost in everything you do in your life is all the guidance you will need to live a harmonious life. This is who you are! When you *know* this about others as well, you are less likely to judge or criticize. You are more likely to accept the Oneness of All. When you fully comprehend what this means, you will understand that what you do to another, you do also to yourself. Some of you will have this understanding while still here in physical form. Others may not remember this knowledge at this time. The important lesson here is to begin to contemplate this Absolute Truth in order to develop your own individual Truth.

Perhaps you are working on a lesson with relationships. It may help you to see that difficulty is present for all in varying forms. You are not alone in your suffering, but you may believe this to be a truth. You are never alone. You may ask for help or guidance at any time, in any place, for any reason. Understand that you are all linked together as One. The benefit to one is benefit to all. The neglect of one is neglect of all. The suffering of one is the suffering of all.

When *one* reaches out to another in Love, *all* are uplifted. Each individual's awareness is linked to the Consciousness of All. If everyone were to practice in their daily living, "do unto others as you would have them do unto you," your world would be the place it was created to be. Even so, when only one lives this Truth, a difference is made for All. This is Truth. This is Love.

I Love You.

eighteen

Light originates from God. It is the sustainer of Life. This is why you say, "God's Healing Light." Light from God permeates every living thing. Every cell. When the Light of God is blocked or cut off, dis-ease occurs. You do not fully understand this process on earth because, even now, you imagine that I speak of light and dark, as you know them.

I speak of My Light as enlightenment, True knowledge of your Oneness with God. This Light comes to you by your choice. Something in your conscious or sub-conscious mind can block this Light, but that is because you have chosen the thoughts that live in your subconscious and conscious mind. It is only your super-conscious mind, your connection to your Source, which is aware.

Your conscious and sub-conscious minds supply your truth to your physical mind. Your super-conscious mind knows only the

Perfection of your creation. Attune to your super-conscious mind to recreate Perfection and Wholeness. Block the thoughts of darkness to let only Light shine within you. The key is in your thoughts. You create with your thoughts.

If there is dis-ease, there is error in your thinking. Weed it out. Get to the root of it. Cultivate your thinking very carefully. Tend your thoughts as carefully as a gardener and watch your health blossom. The choice is yours.

Our connection cannot be broken, but you must choose to connect. The Life Force permeates all living things. It is available to all. The Supply never ends. Ask and you shall receive. Ask knowing that you are already receiving. Change your thinking. Create your life.

I Love You.

nineteen

What would you say to the idea of compassion? What would be your understanding of the word? Many believe that their feelings of sorrow, directed toward the outer circumstances of an individual or group of individuals, comprises having compassion for them. In fact, these same thoughts can reinforce the circumstances you wish to ease. Thought embraced with powerful emotion moves swiftly toward its chosen subject and returns in kind to its owner.

In its higher form, having compassion for someone means that you wish better circumstances for the individual and often those around them. See them in Divine Perfection no matter what the outward appearances may be to the contrary. Envision them in perfect health, emotional harmony, and successful living with circumstances of perfection surrounding every aspect of their life. Your sorrow will create more of the same. Your rejoicing in their better life, even before it manifests in outward appearances, will establish good in their lives and in yours.

There is only Good. Choose to see it in everything. Know that it will manifest, as surely as the Good thoughts that you send out will reach their mark and return to their creator. This is precisely how Blessings flow. Be the one to Bless rather than pity. Choose Good Always. See it in All things. Appearances are only that. What is Real is always Good and it is waiting for someone like you, and you, and you, to reveal It.

I Love You.

TWENTY

Your mind is very powerful. The power rests with your thoughts. What you think, you believe, and what you believe in, you produce. Keep careful watch over your thoughts. They are in your safekeeping and no other's.

Choose to create harmony in your life by carefully choosing what you think. If you were to take one step only toward a better life, this would be the one to take. With care you will soon have a path, which will lead you always in the right direction. There may be loose stones along the way tempting you to stumble. Choose right thinking at every opportunity and your path will widen and brighten with the illumination necessary to always show the way. You will never be lost. You can only be lost in your thoughts. Contemplate this. Your thoughts are your most significant choice. Choose harmonious thoughts and you will create a harmonious life. This is Truth, though you may think it too insignificant to relieve you of your problems.

Your problems have their roots in your thoughts. You must weed them out. Only you can do this. It is your free will, your choice to create a better life for yourself and those around you. Take the first step, which is the first step. Then you will receive all of the help that you ask for. The Power of the Universe is available to help you create a better life. You only have to think it so. This is Truth.

I Love You.

Twenty-one

What matters in an individual's life is his or her personal relationship with the Divine. The name brought forth is of no significance. It is entirely a personal matter. Concern yourself only with the development of the relationship in order that you may have joy and peace and true meaning in your life. There is no substitute. There is only fulfillment or absence. It is your choice.

I do not come unless beckoned. That is the Way. This is Truth. Ask and you shall receive. I Am with you Always, whether you are aware of My Presence or not. You choose your awareness.

The Way is within. Within you, I Am. Quiet your mind. Be still and Know That I Am. Be consistent. Act your intention. Live your life knowing in every moment that I Am with you. Show gratitude by helping others. This is the Way to True Living. Happiness is yours if you choose it and act on it. Think it so. Know it to be True.

I Love You.

TWENTY-TWO

Would you deny another that which you would ask for yourself? Can you imagine a life lived without the need for forgiveness? If that life will be yours you need not consider this further. You would be the Author impressing this thought. You would be Perfection. God Is Perfection.

Always remember that which you give, you receive. It is the same with a thought as it is with an act, which begins with a thought. What you give to others, you will receive. It is the Law of Cause and Effect.

Whether or not the word or the act was intended to harm another is not the point. Do not concern yourself further in order that you may judge or justify. Simply forgive. You have no idea how powerful True Forgiveness is. Unleash it from your heart and you will know. True Forgiveness comes from your heart, not from your head.

Forgive, and then never forget that you have Forgiven. This is the Way. This is True Love and True Love is Absolute Truth in action. Give and you shall receive. Live your life in forgiveness of acts small and large. Yours will be a Life of joy. You will receive the fruits of Spirit. You will have an unburdened heart, and there is no greater Peace.

I Love You.

twenty-three

Peace can be created in your life in the same manner by which the artist creates a masterpiece. You choose peacefulness first with your thoughts. When you intend peace for yourself, you create the energy, or action, necessary to bring it forward, manifested first within your own being. Once established within you, you become a peaceful person. Intending peace for yourself, it is then brought through you and out toward others. Peacefulness directed toward others establishes it firmly in your life.

First, you must choose, and then you must act. This is intention, and human intention is one of the most powerful forces on earth. Intention is another expression for will. Man is created with free will, the ability to choose. The entire universe is behind one person's choice when their intention is strong. This is your "I Am Principle" in action. There is no greater power. You choose whenever you complete the phrase, "I Am____."

It is your choice to intend peace or rage, love or hate, forgiveness or blame, kindness or anger. Your thought is the first step in the emotion expressed. "I Am Love" brings forth a loving countenance. "I Am kind" creates its likeness. "I Am angry" begins with a thought that is easier to change when it is one, before it quickly becomes a cluster of angry thoughts breeding and re-creating in kind with the power of the emotion *you* have given them.

Thought, word, and deed. This is the order of expression. Change negative feelings when they are still in thought, before they become the spoken word, and turn into the act that brings to you the sender, in kind, that which you have created. This is the Way. You can have a peaceful life. It begins with you, as all things do. You must choose. I cannot do this for you. I Am supporting you in *every* choice you make. I created you with free will so that you would have this choice. Choose wisely. Choose Love. Choose Peacefulness.

I Love You.

Twenty-Four

What is Truth versus truth? You are Spiritual beings. This is what you must know. This is who you are. You are also human beings in a physical body: human, being in a physical body. You would say, "I Am Spirit," knowing this Truth. This is Truth because Spirit is everlasting. When you say, "I Am human," this is a truth because it is a temporary matter. One is God Truth and one is human truth.

When you live with God Truth you have Wisdom. When you live with human truth you call it intellect. God Truth can make an enormous difference in your life. Human truth is temporary and continually changes, depending on what you experience with your physical senses. God Truth is an experience of Soul; human truth is an experience of personality.

Humans have expressed Truth knowingly and unknowingly with the saying "wise old soul." Wisdom rings True to you on an intuitive or Soul level. Intellect passes with each new discovery and appeals to a capricious human mind. Wisdom endures, intellect passes away. Choose Wisdom, in all ways.

I Love You.

Twenty-Five

Healing is Divine, Spiritual. It matters not the method. I use a surgeon's hand, a chemist's pill, a layman's hand. I use a willing instrument, the patient's mind, their connection to Me. The first order is to right the thought pattern. Ask knowing that I have already Given, because that which you ask for is already so.

The body responds to thought commands originating in the mind. Believe something to be true and it is. That is the nature of your mind. It is your body's nature to respond. Nature is created in My Perfection. This means human nature as well.

It is human thought that creates. You create for yourselves and those around you. You "hold them in your thoughts." All things are possible. Choose your thoughts carefully. Choose healthy thoughts in every way. You will be at ease in your thinking. There will be no thought of dis-ease. Your body responds automatically. Every cell receives a command and acts on it.

It is easier to correct one mistaken thought before a chain reaction. It is easier to maintain health before disruptive thoughts enter in. It is never too late. Go within, and choose your thoughts. You and only you know what is right for you. Focus your thoughts on the positive at all times. Choose each thought as one that is bringing health forward in your body. Create your health without ceasing.

Re-mind others around you concerning their thoughts directed to you. Envision perfect health specific to what you are creating. Be grateful for all that is good in your life. No one is without goodness in his or her life. Look for goodness everywhere and notice how it multiplies. It will be so because you are creating it. Carefully remove all feelings of anger, hatred, regret, and criticism. Replace them with feelings of peace, love, forgiveness, and gratitude. Hold your focus.

Quiet your mind. Choose your thoughts. You are made in the likeness of your Creator. Place your thoughts on Me. They will be in safekeeping. Know that this is True. You and I are One. You are never alone. Fear does not exist except as it is created in the mind, in your thoughts. Place your thoughts on Love. Give them over to Me.

I Love You.

twenty-six

Remember…

Rest your thoughts with Me.
We are a partnership.
You are never alone.
You create your life.
You can choose peace, for yourself and others.
Be kind.
Thoughts matter.
Words matter.
Deeds matter.
Always, choose Love and Mercy.
Spend quiet moments alone with Me.
Let go of anger, resentment, jealousy, criticism, judgment.
Embrace Peace, Love, Harmony, Kindness, Joy.
Be grateful.
Listen to Nature.
Trust.

Believe in yourself and you believe in Me.
Know that we are One.
Change your thoughts, change your life.
You are Spirit.
You are a Spiritual being having a physical, sensory experience.
You are One with *every* living thing in the Universe.
When one is harmed, all are harmed.
When one is uplifted, all are uplifted.
What you give, you receive.
The giver and receiver are One.
There is only Love.
Love Is All That Is.
God and I Am are One.

I Love You.
Peace Be with you.
So Be It.

twenty-seven

The Soul yearns for Divine connection between God and the physical self. Higher Self is a name that is used to illustrate Divine connection. It is a term that assists some with the understanding of the world beyond the physical one. It depends on the individual's understanding of spiritual matters, as to how closely the term applies. It is your understanding that makes it so. Words are a cumbersome way of teaching. Thought impression leaves little room for error.

Thought impression is the method used on the Spiritual plane of existence. You will discover that all Truths are known in this way. There are no half-truths offered. Each one must discover this to be True. Seek and you shall find. Ask and you shall receive. All Truths will be known by all. True Life will begin Anew.

I Love You.

Twenty-eight

When in need of Love, where do you go? Turn inward, not outside of yourself to find the Love that you are searching for. Self-love is the foundation of romantic love. How can you truly love another if you do not love yourself? You cannot love truly, as a child loves, or to the extent that you are capable, without loving yourself. "Do unto others as you would do unto yourself" means Goodness and Love for all, including yourself.

No longer believe what others tell you about your nature. No longer accept that you have to remain the way you are, if you strive to be different. Change your mind. Create a new image of yourself within your thoughts. Let go of all beliefs and patterns that no longer serve your best interests. Keep your goal always at the forefront of your mind. Look to others for inspiration, but take your guidance from within. Be patient. Be calm. Be steady. Be assured of your success. Be grateful when the change occurs. Be careful not to fall back into old patterns of self-criticism and doubt. Replace all thoughts of disharmony with positive ones and believe in what you tell yourself is True.

I Am here to help. I Am here to Love. I Am Love. I Abide in you. This Is Truth. Trust That It Is So. Believe in Me. Believe in your Self.

I Love You.

twenty-nine

There will be a time of rejoicing in the knowledge that like attracts like. When the minds and the hearts of mankind are unified. When harmony overrides chaos. When Life is as it was intended to be.

What of nature and how it runs its course? Just as you change only in form when you die away from this life, all things change and evolve. Life Is. Hold your thoughts to those of a Higher Nature. All others will die away. You give your thoughts life with your focus of attention. Stay in the moment. Choose the one thought, others of like form will follow. This is key to harmony and a life of satisfaction.

I Am with you always, but your thoughts may lead you to believe that I Am absent, or that you will be unable to reach Me. The connection can never be broken, unless you choose it. You must know this to be Truth.

What you do unto yourself and others, you do also unto Me. You know this Truth, you need only to remember who you are.

I Love You.

Thirty

I Am here, always. Remember, the connection cannot be broken. You need only to send out the thought to "be with Me," as you would say, and It is So. Tell everyone this. What a difference would be made if all believed this Truth.

Less fear in the world brings more Love. It is Love that is needed by all. Love is like air and water and nourishment. You call lack of love failure to thrive, as when a baby does not know that it is loved. I say it in this way because, if you do not know My Love, it is as if it does not exist. You are likened to those babes. Love heals all. I do not speak here of romantic love, for which so many of you search endlessly. That is the lesser form of Love, the form you feel with your physical senses.

Many have not yet learned to experience Reality, which is beyond the physical senses.

This is where the experience of pure, unconditional Love exists. This is My Love. There is no substitute. Everything else in your life is in addition to this Truth. Begin by opening your heart and mind to this possibility. Every single living thing has had an experience of It at some time. It is always there, you need only to remember to call It forth again.

See beauty in all of Creation, including your fellow man. Look for it everywhere. Look without ceasing. Hold the focus of your thoughts. This is how you create. Holding your thoughts on Me, and seeing beauty in all of Creation, brings that which you image to you. This is how you were made in My Likeness. You are a creator and a co-creator with Me. This is Truth. You and I are One. Believe and you will be made Whole, not by Me, but by You, God Who Lives and Breathes within you.

I Love You.

Thirty-one

It is not what you do, but who you become as you go through life's journey that is of importance. You have greater effect on the world as a whole with the quality of your thoughts, than the acts of your hands. Thought, word, and deed, in that order, because they go from far-reaching to local, in their effect or impact. The power of your mind is far-reaching. Your mind can be put to good purpose no matter where you are. The mind has the ability to travel vast distances, impossible for most to consider physically. The mind "travels" at the speed of thought which your science knows yet so little of. The opportunity for vast world change rests in the power of the mind.

Just as the power of the wave rests in the stillness within its depth, before the power is expressed in the form of the wave you see, this *same* power rests within your mind, waiting for you to bring it forward into physical expression. It is your choice. You choose whether or not to open your thoughts to the possibility of this Truth. You choose whether or not to express this Truth, and then, you choose how to express Truth. Your outward expression of your inward thoughts carries with it the character of your Inner Truth.

What you think is what you believe. What you believe is your truth. God-centered thoughts are Truth. God Is Truth. Human-centered thoughts are nothing more or less than what you believe to be true. One is personal truth, the other Universal Truth, God Truth. Choose your thoughts wisely. This is True Power. Power over no other, Power over your self. Power to Be your True Self.

I Love You.

Thirty-Two

It is the intention behind the request that matters most with prayer. Mouthing the words of a prayer that holds little meaning in your heart shows itself clearly as an unsure request. Ask believing that it is already yours and you will receive. Continued effort on your part, directed toward the cause, is a necessary component.

Thought, word, and deed directed as if the outcome has already taken place is the way to success. Apply these directives to any aspect of your life with which you want help to change for the better. See it in your mind clearly as already taking its proper place in your life. Strengthen your vision with practice. In your every thought and action, consider it accomplished. Do not second-guess. Do not look back upon it with doubt. Do not fear that it is lost. If you do, you have changed that which you had asked for. You have replaced success with failure as your envisioned outcome. If that happens, you may say, "It was not God's will."

In fact, it was your will, because you were created with Supreme Will to choose, in every aspect of your life. It begins with thought. Your will becomes My Will because this is the Divine Law of Creation. Know this to be Truth. Whatever you have focused your attention on will be manifested, whether or not this is your conscious wish. Thought matters. Choose your thoughts carefully. Live in the present. Be mind-full of your chosen outcome. Let all other thoughts drop away. This is the Way to a successful outcome.

I Love You.

Thirty-Three

Guidance can be given only to the extent that it is accepted. Those who close their minds to Higher Truth do so at their own peril. It is as if the Life Force Itself is reduced. It is not living life to your full potential.

Divine design is Perfection. You are created in My Likeness. You may choose My Design, or man's. You alone can choose. You have free will to choose your own reality. I do not choose for you. My Will has already been done. You *are* my Perfect Creation. I await only your recognition of this Truth. True Life awaits you.

Let *all* thoughts which are not of Me fall away. Know this Truth and you will see clearly. Your heart will be Light and will serve as a beacon to all that you meet. Each of you is a teacher, a bearer of Truth, or false-truth. It is your choice. You choose continuously throughout your day and throughout your life. You create your life by what you choose to think. Choose thoughts of health, wealth, joy and laughter, kindness, mercy, patience, and understanding.

Do not judge others; you will only judge yourself. Let each live his or her life without undo criticism. Circumstances are not always as they seem. Be kind, but not submissive. Lend a hand, but know that no one should try to live another's life. Too much charity is the same as none. Examine your motive for offering such help. See clearly your hidden desire. Allow all to live the life chosen by them. Live your chosen life and no other's. Remember this always, in all ways.

Be tolerant of all differences. Each of you is finding your way on different paths. Signposts intended for one will confuse another. As some are lost, others are found. All are found in Truth. Time means *no-thing*, except on earth. Forever is Truth, Truth is forever.

I Love You.

Thirty-four

Because you are not aware of something or do not know about it does not mean that it cannot happen or that it does not exist. There is much that is Real that does not meet the eye. You call those things "mysteries of the universe." They are mysterious only to the one who chooses not to see. The one who says, "unseen forces are at work here," is one who is opening to all possibility. The one who says, "seeing is believing," is blocking that which he would hope to see.

The key lies in your thinking. Thoughts of "all things are possible" bring the greatest benefit. Choose your thoughts carefully on this matter. Nurture those thoughts that have been carefully chosen. Act on these thoughts when the need arises. These steps will establish right thinking firmly within you. This is the beginning. There will be many more choices along the path.

Every moment of every hour of every day, you make choices that affect your life. You are creating your life with what you choose. Everything begins with a thought. Remember this. Try and you will succeed. Diligence is necessary. Practice becomes Principle. Right thinking brings joy to your life and to those around you.

I Love You.

thirty-five

Do not think that one is better than another or that an old Soul is preferable to a new One. These are ideas created in man's mind, explanations you give yourselves to try and make sense of the unseen or unknown. Every path is different. Each Soul is unique. Every Soul chooses the life that will bring it closer to the One.

No one can know another's journey. Do not be blinded by appearances or concern yourself with the desire to be like another. To do this is to attempt to live another's life and not your own.

No-thing is as it seems when you perceive by sense only. Mysteries of the universe are made known to every Soul at the time that Soul knows it is appropriate. Every thing has its own season, waxing and waning, giving and receiving. It is the same with nature and with human nature. All Is One.

Let your Soul sing. Seek joy for the sake of joy. Live your life Truly. This is your life, the one you have chosen to live. Listen to your intuition, your inner guidance. Change what you feel is out of balance in your life. Learn to be Peaceful. Seek quiet moments to receive answers, your Truth.

You came here to live this life, at this time. Everything you need to know is within you. You did come with instructions. Your path is unique to you and only you. You need only to remember. Quiet your mind. The answers will come. You must be open to all possibility to receive Truly. Know that the answer may have been in front of you always, or may seem to you too good to be true.

Rest your thoughts with Me. Sincerely seek your Truth and you will receive. Trust in yourself as I Trust in you. Know that you are a powerful Soul first, and the seemingly frail human body that you perceive through your senses, second. When you say that something is "second nature" to you, you are often experiencing your inner Self, which is truly your "first nature." Do not judge others. Concern yourself with being the best that *you* can be. Follow your Inner Guidance. Trust and It Will Be So. Find your Truth.

I Love You.

Thirty-six

Where you are, I Am also. This is So for those who believe that It is So. It is a choice. Whatever will be is truth according to your beliefs. Believe in yourself, and all things are possible to come to you. Believe more in another than in yourself, and you live your life wishing for another's life. Wishing for another's life leaves your own life empty, barren. A fruitless life leads to despondency. In despondency, there is denial. Denial of what led to the despondency is the root of a new Tree of Life to be planted by you.

Look to the cause of unhappiness in your life without blame or envy of others. The cause is in your thinking. Your thoughts lead you to what you believe. Change your thoughts to believe in yourself. Live your own life and no one else's.

Joy will replace despondency. Love will flow into and from your very being, into your life and the lives of those around you. Your life will bear the fruits of Spirit and you will Live in joy forever. Trust and It Will Be So. Believe and It Will Become.

I Love You.

thirty-seven

I Am the Truth, the Light, the Way. Trust in Me and you will lack no-thing. You are created in My Likeness. You are each Sacred Souls. Some may embrace this concept, but few actually Live It.

Do not recite idle words directed toward Me. Talk to Me, and then listen for My guidance. Act on your own behalf. Do not sit and wait for Me or My Angels or your "dead" ancestors or anyone else to change your life for you.

You are the author of your own life, no other. There are no victims. Each and every one, no matter outward appearances, came into this life with a Divine Plan and the tools needed to fulfill this Plan. This *is* your life. There are no substitutes waiting in the wings to play your role. Stop excusing yourself, or asking others to do the same, for anything that blocks you from your heart's goal. I do not mean your romantic heart's notions. I mean your Soul's urging. They are sometimes opposites, but in any case vastly different impressions.

You must ask for help. You must listen and act on the Guidance received. It will always come in a way that is in your highest good and the highest good of others. If you understand it to be other than this, you are deceiving yourself and not receiving My Truth.

Act with kind intention toward every living thing. Harm no other. Allow others to fulfill their Plan. Do not judge. All Will Be Well. My Love Guides All.

I Love You.

Thirty-eight

Listen only to Me. Others are confused by their own experiences, which clouds their understanding of My Truth. I say to you, listen only to Me.

Each individual life expression has its own connection to Me, its Source. The connection is never broken. This is not possible. Even when the Life Force ceases to flow through the physical being, the Spiritual connection shall remain. This is So. There is no other Truth.

Come directly to Me for your Guidance. This is the secret to everlasting Peace, Joy, Love, and Understanding. It remains secret only to those from whom it is hidden—hidden by their own thoughts.

Many of you choose to awaken to Truth at this time. This helps others to find their Way as well. There is no special place or posture or time as you know it to come closer to Me.

I Am available to All, at All times, in All ways. This is Truth. This is the Light of Understanding. This is the Way to Happiness. Be Still, and Know That I Am God.

I Love You.

Thirty-nine

I ask of my Creator
that which I know I must co-create
within my own mind and heart,
and I Am assured of my result.

FORTY

A moment, a day, a week, a month, a year, a life make. Discipline is behavior that is learned. You can apply discipline to your mind and change your behavior one day at a time, even moment to moment. Moments link together to make days, and days to weeks and weeks to months and months to years.

The key is your intention and your focus. Your mind is the seat of your power to change whatever it is in your life that you wish to change. Your will reigns supreme over all. Your will is your freedom to choose. What you will is expressed to Spirit. You can choose to have the Power of the Universe behind your will by focusing your intention. What your mind dwells upon, you will create. What is given out will return, in like form, to its sender. You will receive that which you give.

Time is of no significance beyond your world. The perfect experience for you to see or to know your Self, through the effects of your own actions and reactions, is perfectly created. Time is not important. What is important is your Soul's growth through the experience of knowing Its Self.

You call these experiences "difficult lessons." You may say, "God gives us only that which we can bear." Using the word God here is inaccurate. This wrong thought comes from your human understanding or human truth. This is not Truth. God has given you Life. God sustains all Life. You create your life. You give *yourself* that which you can bear, in order that you can grow from self into Self.

As a child sees, you see your circumstances. No child knows all. Every child must learn. You are as a child in this way, even when you grow old physically. Your Soul seeks all-ways to learn. It seeks Wisdom and Truth, not knowledge, nor that which appears to be truth.

Discipline your mind by carefully choosing your thoughts. Focus your intention. Change your life. Know that the Law of Cause and Effect Is, and learn Truth from the application of this Law in your life.

I Love You.

About the Author

Kathryn Adams Shapiro lives with her husband Ron on a farm in north Baltimore County, Maryland.

Kathryn works privately, as a spiritual healer, with people of all faiths and lack of faith who are given "no hope" by the medical profession. She also works through intercessory prayer with others in need.

Kathryn identifies her work with no single religion, believing instead that Truth can be found in all religions.

People are invited to send prayer requests for healing to:

Kathryn Adams Shapiro
P.O. Box 1374
Brooklandville, MD 21022

BEYOND WORDS PUBLISHING, INC.

OUR CORPORATE MISSION

Inspire to Integrity

OUR DECLARED VALUES

We give to all of life as life has given us.
We honor all relationships.
Trust and stewardship are integral to fulfilling dreams.
Collaboration is essential to create miracles.
Creativity and aesthetics nourish the soul.
Unlimited thinking is fundamental.
Living your passion is vital.
Joy and humor open our hearts to growth.
It is important to remind ourselves of love.